CELEBRATION

by Harold Pinter

samuelfrench.co.uk

Copyright © 1999, 2002 by Harold Pinter
All Rights Reserved

CELEBRATION is fully protected under the copyright laws of the British Commonwealth, including Canada, the United States of America, and all other countries of the Copyright Union. All rights, including professional and amateur stage productions, recitation, lecturing, public reading, motion picture, radio broadcasting, television and the rights of translation into foreign languages are strictly reserved.

ISBN 978-0-573-11283-6

www.samuelfrench.co.uk

www.samuelfrench.com

For Amateur Production Enquiries

United Kingdom and World
excluding North America
plays@samuelfrench.co.uk
020 7255 4302/01

Each title is subject to availability from Samuel French,
depending upon country of performance.

CAUTION: Professional and amateur producers are hereby warned that *CELEBRATION* is subject to a licensing fee. Publication of this play does not imply availability for performance. Both amateurs and professionals considering a production are strongly advised to apply to the appropriate agent before starting rehearsals, advertising, or booking a theatre. A licensing fee must be paid whether the title is presented for charity or gain and whether or not admission is charged.

The professional rights in this play are controlled by Judy Daish Associates Ltd, 2 St Charles Pl, London W10 6EG.

No one shall make any changes in this title for the purpose of production. No part of this book may be reproduced, stored in a retrieval system, or transmitted in any form, by any means, now known or yet to be invented, including mechanical, electronic, photocopying, recording, videotaping, or otherwise, without the prior written permission of the publisher. No one shall upload this title, or part of this title, to any social media websites.

The right of Harold Pinter to be identified as author of this work has been asserted in accordance with Section 77 of the Copyright, Designs and Patents Act 1988.

THINKING ABOUT PERFORMING A SHOW?

There are thousands of plays and musicals available to perform from Samuel French right now, and applying for a licence is easier and more affordable than you might think

From classic plays to brand new musicals, from monologues to epic dramas, there are shows for everyone.

Plays and musicals are protected by copyright law so if you want to perform them, the first thing you'll need is a licence. This simple process helps support the playwright by ensuring they get paid for their work, and means that you'll have the documents you need to stage the show in public.

Not all our shows are available to perform all the time, so it's important to check and apply for a licence before you start rehearsals or commit to doing the show.

LEARN MORE & FIND THOUSANDS OF SHOWS

Browse our full range of plays and musicals and find out more about how to license a show
www.samuelfrench.co.uk/perform

Talk to the friendly experts in our Licensing team for advice on choosing a show, and help with licensing
plays@samuelfrench.co.uk   020 7387 9373

Acting Editions
BORN TO PERFORM

Playscripts designed from the ground up to work the way you do in rehearsal, performance and study

Larger, clearer text for easier reading

Wider margins for notes

Performance features such as character and props lists, sound and lighting cues, and more

+ CHOOSE A SIZE AND STYLE TO SUIT YOU

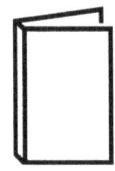

STANDARD EDITION

Our regular paperback book at our regular size

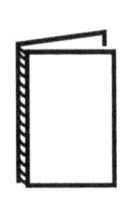

SPIRAL-BOUND EDITION

The same size as the Standard Edition, but with a sturdy, easy-to-fold, easy-to-hold spiral-bound spine

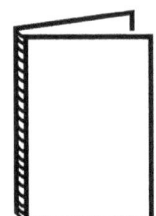

LARGE EDITION

A4 size and spiral bound, with larger text and a blank page for notes opposite every page of text. Perfect for technical and directing use

| LEARN MORE | samuelfrench.co.uk/actingeditions

**Other plays by HAROLD PINTER
published and licensed by Samuel French**

The Birthday Party

The Caretaker

The Dumb Waiter

Family Voices (from the collection *Other Places*)

The Homecoming

A Kind of Alaska (from the collection *Other Places*)

The Lover

Mixed Doubles

Mountain Language

A Night Out

One for the Road (from the collection *Other Places*)

One to Another

The Room

A Slight Ache

Victoria Station (from the collection *Other Places*)

**Other plays by HAROLD PINTER
licensed by Samuel French**

Apart from That

Ashes to Ashes

The Basement

Betrayal

The Black and White

The Dwarfs

The Hothouse

Landscape

Last To Go

Monologue

Moonlight

The New World Order

Night School

No Man's Land

Old Times

Party Time

Precisely

Press Conference

Request Stop

Silence

Tess

That's All

That's Your Trouble

Trouble in the Works

FIND PERFECT PLAYS TO PERFORM AT
www.samuelfrench.co.uk/perform

ABOUT THE AUTHOR

Harold Pinter was born in London in 1930. He lived with Antonia Fraser from 1975 until his death on Christmas Eve 2008. (They were married in 1980).

After studying at the Royal Academy of Dramatic Art and the Central School of Speech and Drama, he worked as an actor under the stage name David Baron. Following his success as a playwright, he continued to act under his own name, on stage and screen. He last acted in 2006 when he appeared in Beckett's *Krapp's Last Tape* at the Royal Court Theatre, directed by Ian Rickson.

He wrote twenty-nine plays including *The Birthday Party, The Dumb Waiter, A Slight Ache, The Hothouse, The Caretaker, The Collection, The Lover, The Homecoming, Old Times, No Man's Land, Betrayal, A Kind of Alaska, One For The Road, The New World Order, Moonlight* and *Ashes to Ashes*. Sketches include *The Black and White, Request Stop, That's your Trouble, Night, Precisely, Apart From that* and the recently rediscovered, *Umbrellas*.

He directed twenty-seven theatre productions, including James Joyce's *Exiles*, David Mamet's *Oleanna*, seven plays by Simon Gray (one of which was *Butley* in 1971 which he directed the film of three years later) and many of his own plays including his last, *Celebration*, paired with his first, *The Room* at The Almeida Theatre, London in the spring of 2000.

He wrote twenty-one screenplays including *The Pumpkin Eater, The Servant, The Go-Between, The French Lieutenant's Woman* and *Sleuth*.

In 2005 he received the Nobel Prize for Literature. Other awards include the Companion of Honour for services to Literature, the Legion D'Honneur, the European Theatre Prize the Laurence Olivier Award and the Moliere D'Honneur for lifetime achievement. In 1999 he was made a Companion of Literature by the Royal Society of Literature. Harold Pinter was awarded eighteen honorary degrees.

MUSIC USE NOTE

Licensees are solely responsible for obtaining formal written permission from copyright owners to use copyrighted music in the performance of this play and are strongly cautioned to do so. If no such permission is obtained by the licensee, then the licensee must use only original music that the licensee owns and controls. Licensees are solely responsible and liable for all music clearances and shall indemnify the copyright owners of the play and their licensing agent, Samuel French, against any costs, expenses, losses and liabilities arising from the use of music by licensees.

IMPORTANT BILLING AND CREDIT REQUIREMENTS

All producers of *CELEBRATION must* give credit to the Author of the Play in all programs distributed in connection with performances of the Play, and in all instances in which the title of the Play appears for the purposes of advertising, publicizing or otherwise exploiting the Play and/or a production. The name of the Author *must* appear on a separate line on which no other name appears, immediately following the title and *must* appear in size of type not less than fifty percent of the size of the title type.

Billing must be substanially as follows:

(NAME OF PRODUCER)
Presents

CELEBRATION

by Harold Pinter

CELEBRATION

by

Harold Pinter

was first presented by the Almeida Theatre Company at the Almeida Theatre, London, on 16 March 2000.

Cast:

LAMBERT	Keith Allen
JULIE	Susan Wooldridge
MATT	Andy de la Tour
PRUE	Lindsay Duncan
RUSSELL	Steven Pacey
SUKI	Lia Williams
RICHARD	Thomas Wheatley
WAITER	Danny Dyer
SONIA	Indira Varma
WAITRESS 1	Nina Raine
WAITRESS 2	Katherine Tozer

Directed by Harold Pinter
Designer: Eileen Diss
Lighting: Mark Hughes
Costume: Dany Everett
Sound: John Leonard

CHARACTERS

LAMBERT
JULIE } all in their forties
MATT
PRUE

RUSSELL, a man in his thirties

SUKI, a woman of twenty-eight

RICHARD, a man in his fifties

WAITER, a man of twenty-five

SONIA, a woman in her thirties

TABLE ONE

SCENE: *A restaurant. Two curved banquettes.* **LAMBERT**, **JULIE**, **MATT**, *and* **PRUE** *sit at one banquette,* **RUSSELL** *and* **SUKI** *at the other.*

WAITER Who's having the duck?

LAMBERT The duck's for me.

JULIE No it isn't.

LAMBERT No it isn't. Who's it for?

JULIE Me.

LAMBERT What am I having? I thought I was having the duck.

JULIE *(to* **WAITER***)* The duck's for me.

MATT *(to* **WAITER***)* Chicken for my wife, steak for me.

WAITER Chicken for the lady.

PRUE Thank you so much.

WAITER And who's having the steak?

MATT Me. *(He picks up a wine bottle and pours)* Here we are. Frascati for the ladies. And Valpolicella for me.

LAMBERT And for me. I mean, what about me? What did I order? I haven't the faintest idea. What did I order?

JULIE Who cares?

LAMBERT Who cares? I bloody care.

PRUE Osso buco.

LAMBERT Osso what?

PRUE Buco.

MATT It's an old Italian dish.

LAMBERT I knew *osso* was Italian but I know bugger-all about *bucco*.

MATT I didn't know arsehole was Italian.

LAMBERT Yes, but on the other hand what's the Italian for arsehole?

PRUE Julie, Lambert Happy anniversary.

MATT Cheers.

They lift their glasses and drink.

TABLE TWO

RUSSELL They believe in me.

SUKI Who do?

RUSSELL They do. What do you mean, who do? They do.

SUKI Oh, do they?

RUSSELL Yes, they believe in me. They reckon me. They're investing in me. In my *nous*. They believe in me.

SUKI Listen. I believe in you. Honestly. I do. No really, honestly. I'm sure they believe in you. And they're right to believe in you. I mean, listen, I want you to be rich, believe me. I want you to be rich so that you can buy me houses and panties and I'll know that you really love me.

They drink.

RUSSELL Listen, she was just a secretary. That's all. No more.

SUKI Like me.

RUSSELL What do you mean like you? She was nothing like you.

SUKI I was a secretary once.

RUSSELL She was a scrubber. A scrubber. They're all the same, these secretaries, these scrubbers. They're like politicians. They love power, they use it. They go home, they get on the phone, they tell their girlfriends, they have a good laugh. Listen to me. I'm being honest. You won't find many like me. I fell for it. I've admitted it. She just twisted me round her little finger.

SUKI That's funny. I thought she twisted you round *your* little finger.

Pause.

RUSSELL You don't know what these girls are like. Those secretaries.

SUKI Oh I think I do.

RUSSELL You don't.

SUKI Oh I do.

RUSSELL What do you mean, you do?

SUKI I've been behind a few filing cabinets.

RUSSELL What?

SUKI In my time. When I was a plump young secretary. I know what the back of a filing cabinet looks like.

RUSSELL Oh, do you?

SUKI Oh yes. Listen, I would invest in you myself if I had any money. Do you know why? Because I believe in you.

RUSSELL What's all this about filing cabinets?

SUKI Oh, that was when I was a plump young secretary. I would never do all those things now. Never. Out of the question. You see, the trouble was I was so excitable, their excitement made me so excited, but I would never do all those things now I'm a grown-up woman and not a silly young thing, a silly and dizzy young girl, such a naughty, saucy, flirty, giggly young thing; sometimes I could hardly walk from one filing cabinet to another I was so excited, I was so plump and wobbly it was terrible, men simply couldn't keep their hands off me, their demands were outrageous but coming back to more important things, they're right to believe in you; why shouldn't they believe in you?

TABLE ONE

JULIE I've always told him. Always. But he doesn't listen. I tell him all the time. But he doesn't listen.

PRUE You mean he just doesn't listen?

JULIE I tell him all the time.

PRUE *(to* **LAMBERT***)* Why don't you listen to your wife? She stands by you through thick and thin. You've got a loyal wife there and never forget it.

LAMBERT I've got a loyal wife where?

PRUE Here! At this table.

LAMBERT I've got one under the table, take my tip. *(He looks under the table)* Christ. She's really loyal under the table. Always has been. You wouldn't believe it.

JULIE Why don't you go and buy a new car and drive it into a brick wall?

LAMBERT She loves me.

MATT No, she loves new cars.

LAMBERT With soft leather seats.

MATT There was a song once.

LAMBERT How did it go?

MATT
"AIN'T SHE NEAT?
AIN'T SHE NEAT?
AS SHE'S WALKING UP THE STREET.
SHE'S GOT A LOVELY BUBBLY PAIR OF TITS
AND A SOFT LEATHER SEAT."

LAMBERT That's a really beautiful song.

MATT I've always admired that song. You know what it is? It's a traditional folk song.

LAMBERT It's got class.

MATT It's got tradition and class.

LAMBERT They don't grow on trees.

MATT Too bloody right.

LAMBERT Hey, Matt!

MATT What?

> **LAMBERT** *picks up the bottle of Valpolicella. It is empty.*

LAMBERT There's something wrong with this bottle.

> **MATT** *turns and calls.*

MATT Waiter!

TABLE TWO

RUSSELL All right. Tell me. Do you think I have a nice character?

SUKI Yes, I think you do. I think you do. I mean I think you do. Well... I mean... I think you could have quite a nice character but the trouble is that when you come down to it you haven't actually got any character to begin with – I mean as such, that's the thing.

RUSSELL As such?

SUKI Yes, the thing is you haven't really got any character at all, have you? As such. *Au fond*. But I wouldn't worry about it. For example, look at me. I don't have any character either. I'm just a reed. I'm just a reed in the wind. Aren't I? You know I am. I'm just a reed in the wind.

RUSSELL You're a whore.

SUKI A whore in the wind.

RUSSELL With the wind blowing up your skirt.

SUKI That's right. How did you know? How did you know the sensation? I didn't know that men could possibly know about that kind of thing. I mean men don't wear skirts. So I didn't think men could possibly know what it was like when the wind blows up a girl's skirt. Because men don't wear skirts.

RUSSELL You're a prick.

SUKI Not quite.

RUSSELL You're a prick.

SUKI Good gracious. Am I really?

RUSSELL Yes. That's what you are really.

SUKI Am I really?

RUSSELL Yes. That's what you are really.

TABLE ONE

LAMBERT What's the other song you know? The one you said was a classic.

MATT
  "WASH ME IN THE WATER
  WHERE YOU WASHED YOUR DIRTY DAUGHTER."

LAMBERT That's it. *(To* **JULIE***:)* Know that one?

JULIE It's not in my repertoire, darling.

LAMBERT This is the best restaurant in town. That's what they say.

MATT That's what they say.

LAMBERT This is a piss-up dinner. Do you know how much money I made last year?

MATT I know this is a piss-up dinner.

LAMBERT It is a piss-up dinner.

PRUE *(to* **JULIE***)* His mother always hated me. The first time she saw me she hated me. She never gave me one present in the whole of her life. Nothing. She wouldn't give me the drippings off her nose.

JULIE I know.

PRUE The drippings off her nose. Honestly.

JULIE All mothers-in-law are like that. They love their sons. They love their boys. They don't want their sons to be fucked by other girls. Isn't that right?

PRUE Absolutely. All mothers want their sons to be fucked by themselves.

JULIE By their mothers.

PRUE All mothers—

LAMBERT All mothers want to be fucked by their mothers.

MATT Or by themselves.

PRUE No, you've got it the wrong way round.

LAMBERT How's that?

MATT All mothers want to be fucked by their sons.

LAMBERT Now wait a minute—

MATT My point is—

LAMBERT No, my point is – how old do you have to be?

JULIE To be what?

LAMBERT To be fucked by your mother.

MATT Any age, mate. Any age.

They all drink.

LAMBERT How did you enjoy your dinner, darling?

JULIE I wasn't impressed.

LAMBERT You weren't impressed?

JULIE No.

LAMBERT I bring her to the best caff in town – spending a fortune – and she's not impressed.

MATT Don't forget this is your anniversary. That's why we're here.

LAMBERT What anniversary?

PRUE It's your wedding anniversary.

LAMBERT All I know is this is the most expensive fucking restaurant in town and she's not impressed.

RICHARD *comes to the table.*

RICHARD Good evening.

MATT Good evening.

PRUE Good evening.

JULIE Good evening.

LAMBERT Good evening, Richard How you been?

RICHARD Very very well. Been to a play?

MATT No. The ballet.

RICHARD Oh, the ballet. What was it?

LAMBERT That's a fucking good question.

MATT It's unanswerable.

RICHARD Good, was it?

LAMBERT Unbelievable.

JULIE What ballet?

MATT None of them could reach the top notes. Could they?

RICHARD Good dinner?

MATT Fantastic.

LAMBERT Top-notch. Gold-plated.

PRUE Delicious.

LAMBERT My wife wasn't impressed.

RICHARD Oh, really?

JULIE I liked the waiter.

RICHARD Which one?

JULIE The one with the fur-lined jockstrap.

LAMBERT He takes it off for breakfast.

JULIE Which is more than you do.

RICHARD Well, how nice to see you all.

PRUE She wasn't impressed with her food. It's true. She said so. She thought it was dry as dust. She said – what did you say, darling? – she's my sister – she said she could cook better than that with one hand stuffed between her legs; she said – no, honestly – she said she could make a better sauce than the one on that plate if she pissed into it. Don't think she was joking – she's my sister, I've known her all my life, all my life, since we were little innocent girls, all our lives, when we were babies, when we used to lie in the nursery and hear Mummy beating the shit out of Daddy. We saw the blood on the sheets the next day – when Nanny was in the pantry – my sister and me – and Nanny was in the pantry – and the pantry maid was in the larder and the parlor maid was in the laundry room washing the blood out of the sheets. That's how my little sister and I were brought up and she could make a better sauce than yours if she pissed into it.

MATT Well, it's lovely to be here, I'll say that.

LAMBERT Lovely to be here.

JULIE Lovely, lovely.

MATT Really lovely.

RICHARD Thank you.

   PRUE *stands and goes to* RICHARD.

PRUE Can I thank you? Can I thank you personally? I'd like to thank you myself, in my own way.

RICHARD Well, thank you.

PRUE No, no, I'd really like to thank you in a very personal way.

JULIE She'd like to give you her personal thanks.

PRUE Will you let me kiss you? I'd like to kiss you on the mouth.

JULIE That's funny. I'd like to kiss him on the mouth too. *(She stands and goes to him)* Because I've been maligned, I've been misrepresented. I never said I didn't like your sauce. I love your sauce.

PRUE We can't both kiss him on the mouth at the same time.

LAMBERT You could tickle his arse with a feather.

RICHARD Well, I'm so glad. I'm really glad. See you later I hope.

RICHARD *goes.* PRUE *and* JULIE *sit. Silence.*

MATT Charming man.

LAMBERT That's why this is the best and most expensive restaurant in the whole of Europe – because he *insists* upon proper standards, he *insists* that standards are maintained up to the highest standards, up to the very highest fucking standards—

MATT He doesn't jib.

LAMBERT Jib? Of course he doesn't jib – it would be more than his life was worth. He jibs at nothing!

PRUE I knew him in the old days.

MATT What do you mean?

PRUE When he was a chef.

LAMBERT*'s mobile phone rings.*

LAMBERT Who the fuck's this? *(He switches it on)* Yes? What? *(He listens briefly)* I said no calls! It's my fucking wedding anniversary! *(He switches it off)* Cunt.

TABLE TWO

SUKI I'm so proud of you.

RUSSELL Yes?

SUKI And I know these people are good people. These people who believe in you. They're good people. Aren't they?

RUSSELL Very good people.

SUKI And when I meet them, when you introduce me to them, they'll treat me with respect, won't they? They won't want to fuck me behind a filing cabinet?

SONIA *comes to the table.*

SONIA Good evening.

RUSSELL Good evening.

SUKI Good evening.

SONIA Everything all right?

RUSSELL Wonderful.

SONIA No complaints?

RUSSELL Absolutely no complaints whatsoever. Absolutely numero uno all along the line.

SONIA What a lovely compliment.

RUSSELL Heartfelt.

SONIA Been to the theatre?

SUKI The opera.

SONIA Oh, really, what was it?

SUKI Well...there was a lot going on. A lot of singing. A great deal, as a matter of fact. They never stopped. Did they?

RUSSELL *(to* SONIA*)* Listen, let me ask you something.

SONIA You can ask me absolutely anything you like.

RUSSELL What was your upbringing?

SONIA That's funny. Everybody asks me that. Everybody seems to find that an interesting subject. I don't know why. Isn't it funny? So many people express curiosity about my upbringing. I've no idea why. What you really mean of course is how did I arrive in the position I hold now – *maîtresse d'hôtel* – isn't that right? Isn't that your question? Well, I was born in Bethnal Green. My mother was a chiropodist. I had no father.

RUSSELL Fantastic.

SONIA Are you going to try our bread-and-butter pudding?

RUSSELL In spades. *(*SONIA *smiles and goes)* Did I ever tell you about my mother's bread-and-butter pudding?

SUKI You never have. Please tell me.

RUSSELL You really want me to tell you? You're not being insincere?

SUKI Darling. Give me your hand. There. I have your hand. I'm holding your hand. Now please tell me. Please tell me about your mother's bread-and-butter pudding. What was it like?

RUSSELL It was like drowning in an ocean of richness.

SUKI How beautiful. You're a poet.

RUSSELL I wanted to be a poet once. But I got no encouragement from my dad. He thought I was an arsehole.

SUKI He was jealous of you, that's all. He saw you as a threat. He thought you wanted to steal his wife.

RUSSELL His wife?

SUKI Well, you know what they say.

RUSSELL What?

SUKI Oh, you know what they say.

The WAITER *comes to the table and pours wine.*

WAITER Do you mind if I interject?

RUSSELL Eh?

WAITER I say, do you mind if I make an interjection?

SUKI We'd welcome it.

WAITER It's just that I heard you talking about T. S. Eliot a little bit earlier this evening.

SUKI Oh, you heard that, did you?

WAITER I did. And I thought you might be interested to know that my grandfather knew T. S. Eliot quite well.

SUKI Really?

WAITER I'm not claiming that he was a close friend of his, but he was a damn sight more that a nodding acquaintance. He knew them all, in fact, Ezra Pound, W. H. Auden, C. Day-Lewis, Louis MacNeice, Stephen Spender, George Barker, Dylan Thomas, and if you go back a few years he was a bit of a drinking companion of D. H. Lawrence, Joseph Conrad, Ford Madox Ford, W. B. Yeats, Aldous Huxley, Virginia Woolf, and Thomas Hardy in his dotage. My grandfather was carving out a niche for himself in politics at the time. Some saw him as a future Chancellor of the Exchequer or at least First Lord of the Admiralty but he decided instead to command a battalion in the Spanish Civil War but as things turned out he spent most of his spare time in the United States where he was a very close pal of Ernest Hemingway – they used to play gin rummy together until the cows came home. But he was also boon compatriots with William Faulkner, Scott Fitzgerald, Upton Sinclair, John Dos Passos – you know, that whole vivid Chicago gang – not to mention John Steinbeck,

Erskine Caldwell, Carson McCullers, and other members of the old Deep South conglomerate. I mean – what I'm trying to say is – that as a man my grandfather was just about as all-round as you can get. He was never without his pocket Bible and he was a dab hand at pocket billiards. He stood four-square in the center of the intellectual and literary life of the tens, twenties, and thirties. He was James Joyce's godmother.

Silence.

RUSSELL Have you been working here long?

WAITER Years.

RUSSELL You going to stay until it changes hands?

WAITER Are you suggesting that I'm about to get the boot?

SUKI They wouldn't do that to a nice lad like you.

WAITER To be brutally honest, I don't think I'd recover if they did a thing like that. This place is like a womb to me. I prefer to stay in my womb. I strongly prefer that to being born.

RUSSELL I don't blame you. Listen, next time we're talking about T. S. Eliot I'll drop you a card.

WAITER You would make me a very happy man. Thank you. Thank you. You are incredibly gracious people.

SUKI How sweet of you.

WAITER Gracious and graceful.

He goes.

SUKI What a nice young man.

TABLE ONE

LAMBERT You won't believe this. You're not going to believe this – I'm only saying this because I'm among friends – and I know I'm well liked because I trust my family and my friends – because I know they like me fundamentally – you know, deep down they trust me, deep down they respect me – otherwise I wouldn't say this. I wouldn't take you all into my confidence if I thought you all hated my guts – I couldn't be open and honest with you if I thought you thought I was a pile of shit. If I thought you would like to see me hung, drawn and fucking quartered – I could never be frank and honest with you if that was the truth – never... *(Silence)* But as I was about to say, you won't believe this. I fell in love once and this girl I fell in love with loved me back. I know she did.

Pause.

JULIE Wasn't that me, darling?

LAMBERT Who?

MATT Her.

LAMBERT Her? No, not her. A girl. I used to take her for walks along the river.

JULIE Lambert fell in love with me on the top of a bus. It was a short journey. Fulham Broadway to Shepherd's Bush, but it was enough. He was trembling all over. I remember. *(To* **PRUE***)* When I got home I came and sat on your bed, didn't I?

LAMBERT I used to take this girl for walks along the river. I was young. I wasn't much more than a nipper.

MATT That's funny. I never knew anything about that. And I knew you quite well, didn't I?

LAMBERT What do you mean you knew me quite well? You knew nothing about me. You know nothing about me. Who the fuck are you anyway?

MATT I'm your big brother.

LAMBERT I'm talking about love, mate. You know, real fucking love, walking along the banks of a river holding hands.

MATT I saw him the day he was born. You know what he looked like? An alcoholic. Pissed as a newt. He could hardly stand.

JULIE He was trembling like a leaf on top of that bus. I'll never forget it.

PRUE I was there when you came home. I remember what you said. You came into my room. You sat down on my bed.

MATT What did she say?

PRUE I mean we were sisters, weren't we?

MATT Well, what did she say?

PRUE I'll never forget what you said. You sat on my bed. Didn't you? Do you remember?

LAMBERT This girl was in love with me – I'm trying to tell you.

PRUE Do you remember what you said?

TABLE TWO

    RICHARD *comes to the table.*

RICHARD Good evening.

RUSSELL Good evening.

SUKI Good evening.

RICHARD Everything in order?

RUSSELL First class.

RICHARD I'm so glad.

SUKI Can I say something?

RICHARD But indeed—

SUKI Everyone is so happy in your restaurant. I mean women and men. You make people so happy.

RICHARD Well, we do like to feel that it's a happy restaurant.

RUSSELL It is a happy restaurant. For example, look at me. Look at me. I'm basically a totally disordered personality; some people would describe me as a psychopath. *(To* SUKI*)* Am I right?

SUKI Yes.

RUSSELL But when I'm sitting in the restaurant I suddenly find I have no psychopathic tendencies at all. I don't feel like killing everyone in sight. I don't feel like putting a bomb under everyone's arse. I feel something quite different. I have a sense of equilibrium, of harmony, I love my fellow diners. Now this is very unusual for me. Normally I feel – as I've just said – absolute malice and hatred towards everyone within spitting distance – but here I feel love. How do you explain it?

SUKI It's the ambience.

RICHARD Yes. I think ambience is that intangible thing that cannot be defined.

RUSSELL Quite right.

SUKI It is intangible. You're absolutely right.

RUSSELL Absolutely.

RICHARD That is absolutely right. But it does – I would freely admit – exist. It's something you find you are part of. Without knowing exactly what it is.

RUSSELL Yes. I had an old schoolmaster once who used to say that ambience surrounds you. He never stopped saying that. He lived in a little house in a nice little village but none of us boys were ever invited to tea.

RICHARD Yes, it's funny you should say that. I was brought up in a little village myself.

SUKI No? Were you?

RICHARD Yes, isn't it odd? In a little village in the country.

RUSSELL What, right in the country?

RICHARD Oh, absolutely. And my father once took me to our village pub. I was only that high. Too young to join him for his pint, of course. But I did look in. Black beams.

RUSSELL On the roof?

RICHARD Well, holding the ceiling up in fact. Old men smoking pipes, no music of course, cheese rolls, gherkins, happiness. I think this restaurant – which you so kindly patronize – was inspired by that pub in my childhood. I do hope you noticed that you have complimentary gherkins as soon as you take your seat.

SUKI That was you! That was your idea!

RICHARD I believe the concept of this restaurant rests in that public house of my childhood.

SUKI I find that incredibly moving.

TABLE ONE

LAMBERT I'd like to raise my glass.

MATT What to?

LAMBERT To my wife. To our anniversary.

JULIE Oh, darling! You remembered!

LAMBERT I'd like to raise my glass. I ask you to raise your glasses to my wife.

JULIE I'm so touched by this, honestly. I mean, I have to say—

LAMBERT Raise your fucking glass and shut up!

JULIE But darling, that's naked aggression. He doesn't normally go in for naked aggression. He usually disguises it under honeyed words. What is it, sweetie? He's got a cold in the nose, that's what it is.

LAMBERT I want us to drink to our anniversary. We've been married for more bloody years than I can remember and it don't seem a day too long.

PRUE Cheers.

MATT Cheers.

JULIE It's funny our children aren't here. When they were young we spent so much time with them, the little things, looking after them.

PRUE I know.

JULIE Playing with them.

PRUE Feeding them.

JULIE Being their mothers.

PRUE They always loved me much more than they loved him.

JULIE Me too. They loved me to distraction. I was their mother.

PRUE Yes, I was too. I was my children's mother.

MATT They have no memory.

LAMBERT Who?

MATT Children. They have no memory. They remember nothing. They don't remember who their father was or who their mother was. It's all a hole in the wall for them. They don't remember their own life.

   SONIA *comes to the table.*

SONIA Everything all right?

JULIE Perfect.

SONIA Were you at the opera this evening?

JULIE No.

PRUE No.

SONIA Theatre?

PRUE No.

JULIE No.

MATT This is a celebration.

SONIA Oh my goodness! A birthday?

MATT Anniversary.

PRUE My sister and her husband. Anniversary of their marriage. I was her leading bridesmaid.

MATT I was his best man.

LAMBERT I was just about to fuck her at the altar when somebody stopped me.

SONIA Really?

MATT I stopped him. His zip went down and I kicked him up the arse. It would have been a scandal. The world's press was on the doorstep.

JULIE He was always impetuous.

SONIA We get so many different kinds of people in here, people from all walks of life.

PRUE Do you really?

SONIA Oh yes. People from all walks of life. People from different countries. I've often said, "You don't have to speak English to enjoy good food." I've often said that. Or even understand English. It's like sex, isn't it? You don't have to be English to enjoy sex. You don't have to speak English to enjoy sex. Lots of people enjoy sex without being English. I've known one or two Belgian people, for example, who love sex and they don't speak a word of English. The same applies to Hungarians.

LAMBERT Yes. I met a chap who was born in Venezuela once and he didn't speak a fucking word of English.

MATT Did he enjoy sex?

LAMBERT Sex?

SONIA Yes, it's funny you should say that. I met a man from Morocco once and he was very interested in sex.

JULIE What happened to him?

SONIA Now you've upset me. I think I'm going to cry.

PRUE Oh, poor dear. Did he let you down?

SONIA He's dead. He died in another woman's arms. He was on the job. Can you see how tragic my life has been?

Pause.

MATT Well, I can. I don't know about the others.

JULIE I can too.

PRUE So can I.

SONIA Have a happy night.

She goes.

LAMBERT Lovely woman.

The WAITER *comes to the table and pours wine into their glasses.*

WAITER Do you mind if I interject?

MATT What?

WAITER Do you mind if I make an interjection.

MATT Help yourself.

WAITER It's just that a little bit earlier I heard you saying something about the Hollywood studio system in the thirties.

PRUE Oh, you heard that?

WAITER Yes. And I thought you might be interested to know that my grandfather was very familiar with a lot of the old Hollywood film stars back in those days. He used to knock about with Clark Gable and Elisha Cook, Jr. and he was one of the very few native-born Englishmen to have had it off with Hedy Lamarr.

JULIE No!

LAMBERT What was she like in the sack?

WAITER He said she was really tasty.

JULIE I'll bet she was.

WAITER Of course there was a very well established Irish Mafia in Hollywood in those days. And there was a very close connection between some of the famous Irish film stars and some of the famous Irish gangsters in Chicago. Al Capone and Victor Mature, for example. The were both Irish. Then there was John Dillinger, the celebrated gangster, and Gary Cooper, the celebrated film star. They were Jewish.

Silence.

JULIE It makes you think, doesn't it?

PRUE It does make you think.

LAMBERT You see the girl at that table? I know her. I fucked her when she was eighteen.

JULIE What, by the banks of the river?

> **LAMBERT** *waves at* **SUKI** **SUKI** *waves back.* **SUKI** *whispers to* **RUSSELL**, *gets up, and goes to* **LAMBERT**'s *table, followed by* **RUSSELL**.

SUKI Lambert! It's you!

LAMBERT Suki! You remember me!

SUKI Do you remember me?

LAMBERT Do I remember you? *Do* I remember you!

SUKI This is my husband, Russell.

LAMBERT Hello, Russell.

RUSSELL Hello, Lambert.

LAMBERT This is my wife, Julie.

JULIE Hello, Suki.

SUKI Hello, Julie.

RUSSELL Hello, Julie.

JULIE Hello, Russell.

LAMBERT And this is my brother, Matt.

MATT Hello, Suki, hello, Russell.

SUKI Hello, Matt.

RUSSELL Hello, Matt.

LAMBERT And this is his wife, Prue. She's Julie's sister.

SUKI She's not!

PRUE Yes, we're sisters and they're brothers.

SUKI They're not!

RUSSELL Hello, Prue.

PRUE Hello, Russell.

SUKI Hello, Prue.

PRUE Hello, Suki.

LAMBERT Sit down. Squeeze in. Have a drink. *(They sit)* What'll you have?

RUSSELL A drop of that red wine would work wonders.

LAMBERT Suki?

RUSSELL She'll have the same.

SUKI *(to* **LAMBERT***)* Are you still obsessed with gardening?

LAMBERT Me?

SUKI *(to* **JULIE***)* When I knew him he was absolutely obsessed with gardening.

LAMBERT Yes, well, I would say I'm still moderately obsessed with gardening.

JULIE He likes grass.

LAMBERT It's true. I love grass.

JULIE Green grass.

SUKI You used to love flowers, didn't you? Do you still love flowers?

JULIE He adores flowers. The other day I saw him emptying a piss pot into a bowl of lilies.

RUSSELL My dad was a gardener.

MATT Not your grandad?

RUSSELL No, my dad.

SUKI That's right, he was. He was always walking about with a lawn mower.

LAMBERT What, even in the Old Kent Road?

RUSSELL He was a man of the soil.

MATT How about your grandad?

RUSSELL I never had one.

JULIE Funny that when you knew my husband you thought he was obsessed with gardening. I always thought he was obsessed with girls' bums.

SUKI Really?

PRUE Oh, yes, he was always a keen wobbler.

MATT What do you mean? How do you know?

PRUE Oh, don't get excited. It's all in the past.

MATT What is?

SUKI I sometimes feel that the past is never past.

RUSSELL What do you mean?

JULIE You mean that yesterday is today?

SUKI That's right. You feel the same, do you?

JULIE I do.

MATT Bollocks.

JULIE I wouldn't like to live again though would you? Once is more than enough.

LAMBERT I'd like to live again. In fact I'm going to make it my job to live again. I'm going to come back as a better person, a more civilized person, a gentler person, a nicer person.

JULIE Impossible.

Pause.

PRUE I wonder where these two met. I mean Lambert and Suki.

RUSSELL Behind a filing cabinet.

Silence.

JULIE What is a filing cabinet?

RUSSELL It's a thing you get behind.

Pause.

LAMBERT No, not me, mate. You've got the wrong bloke. I agree with my wife. I don't even know what a filing cabinet looks like. I wouldn't know a filing cabinet if I met one coming around the corner.

Pause.

JULIE So what's your job now then, Suki?

SUKI Oh, I'm a schoolteacher now. I teach infants.

PRUE What, little boys and little girls?

SUKI What about you?

PRUE Oh, Julie and me – we run charities. We do charities.

RUSSELL Must be pretty demanding work.

JULIE Yes, we're at it day and night, aren't we?

PRUE Well, there are so many worthy causes.

MATT *(to* RUSSELL*)* You're a banker? Right?

RUSSELL That's right

MATT *(to* LAMBERT*)* He's a banker.

LAMBERT With a big future before him.

MATT Well, that's what he reckons.

LAMBERT I want to ask you a question. How did you know he was a banker?

MATT Well, it's the way he holds himself, isn't it?

LAMBERT Oh yes.

SUKI What about you two?

LAMBERT Us two?

SUKI Yes.

LAMBERT Well, we're consultants, Matt and me. Strategy consultants.

MATT Strategy consultants.

LAMBERT It means we don't carry guns. *(*MATT *and* LAMBERT *laugh)* We don't have to!

MATT We're peaceful strategy consultants.

LAMBERT Worldwide. Keeping the peace.

RUSSELL Wonderful.

LAMBERT Eh?

RUSSELL Really impressive. We need a few more of you about. *(Pause)* We need more people like you. Taking responsibility. Taking charge. Keeping the peace. Enforcing the peace. Enforcing peace. We need more like you. I think I'll have a word with my bank. I'm moving any minute to a more substantial bank. I'll have a word with them. I'll suggest lunch. In the City. I know an ideal restaurant. All the waitresses have big tits.

SUKI Aren't you pushing the tits bit a bit far?

RUSSELL Me? I thought you did that.

Pause.

LAMBERT Be careful. You're talking to your wife.

MATT Have some respect, mate.

LAMBERT Have respect. That's all we ask.

MATT It's not much to ask.

LAMBERT But it's crucial.

Pause.

RUSSELL So how is the strategic consultancy business these days?

LAMBERT Very good, old boy. Very good.

MATT Very good. We're at the receiving end of some of the best tea in China.

> RICHARD *and* SONIA *come to the table with a magnum of champagne, the* WAITER *with a tray of glasses. Everyone gasps.*

RICHARD To celebrate a treasured wedding anniversary.

> MATT *looks at the label on the bottle.*

MATT That's the best of the best.

> *The bottle opens.* RICHARD *pours.*

LAMBERT And may the best man win!

JULIE The woman always wins.

PRUE Always.

SUKI That's really good news.

PRUE The woman always wins.

> RICHARD *and* SONIA *raise their glasses.*

RICHARD To the happy couple. God bless. God bless you all.

EVERYONE Cheers. Cheers...

MATT What a wonderful restaurant this is.

SONIA Well, we do care. I will say that. We care. That's the point. Don't we?

RICHARD Yes. We do care. We care about the welfare of our clientele. I will say that.

> LAMBERT *stands and goes to them.*

LAMBERT What you say means so much to me. Let me give you a cuddle. *(He cuddles* RICHARD*)* And let me give you a cuddle. *(He cuddles* SONIA*)* This is so totally rare, you see. None of this normally happens. People normally – you know – people normally are so distant from each other. That's what I've found. Take a given bloke – this given bloke – this given bloke doesn't know that another given bloke exists. It goes down through history, doesn't it?

MATT It does.

LAMBERT One bloke doesn't know that another bloke exists. Generally speaking. I've often noticed.

SONIA *(to* JULIE *and* PRUE*)* I'm so touched that you're sisters. I had a sister. But she married a foreigner and I haven't seen her since.

PRUE Some foreigners are all right.

SONIA Oh, I think foreigners are charming. Most people in this restaurant tonight are foreigners. My sister's husband had a lot of charm but he also had an enormous mustache. I had to kiss him at the wedding. I can't describe how awful it was. I've got such soft skin, you see.

WAITER Do you mind if I interject?

RICHARD I'm sorry?

WAITER Do you mind if I make an interjection?

RICHARD What on earth do you mean?

WAITER Well, it's just that I heard all these people talking about the Austro-Hungarian Empire a little while ago and I wondered if they'd ever heard about my grandfather. He was an incredibly close friend of the Archduke himself and he once had a cup of tea with Benito Mussolini. They all played poker together, Winston Churchill included. The funny thing about my grandfather was that the palms of his hands always seemed to be burning. But his eyes were elsewhere. He had a really strange life. He was in love, he told me once, with the woman who turned out to be my grandmother, but he lost her somewhere. She disappeared, I think, in a sandstorm. In the desert. My grandfather was everything men aspired to be in those days. He was tall, dark and handsome. He was full of goodwill. He'd even give a cripple with no legs crawling on his belly through the slush and mud of a country lane a helping hand. He'd lift him up, he'd show him his way, he'd point him in the right direction. He was like Jesus Christ in that respect. And he was gregarious. He loved the society of his fellows, W. B. Yeats. T. S. Eliot, Igor Stravinsky, Picasso, Ezra Pound, Bertolt Brecht, Don Bradman, the Beverly Sisters, the Inkspots, Franz Kafka, and the Three Stooges. He knew these people where they were isolated, where they were alone, where they fought against savage and pitiless odds, where they suffered vast wounds to their bodies, their bellies, their legs, their trunks, their eyes, their throats, their breasts, their balls—

LAMBERT *(standing)* Well, Richard – what a great dinner!

RICHARD I'm so glad.

LAMBERT *opens his wallet and unpeels fifty-pound notes. He gives two to* RICHARD.

LAMBERT This is for you.

RICHARD No, no really—

LAMBERT No, no, this is for you. *(To* SONIA*)* And this is for you.

SONIA Oh, no, please—

LAMBERT *dangles the notes in front of her cleavage.*

LAMBERT Shall I put them down here? *(*SONIA *giggles)* No, I'll tell you what – you wearing suspenders? *(*SONIA *giggles)* Stick them in your suspenders. *(To* WAITER*)* Here you are, son. Mind how you go. *(Puts a note into his pocket)* Great dinner. Great restaurant. Best in the country.

MATT Best in the world, I'd say.

LAMBERT Exactly. *(To* **RICHARD***)* I'm taking their bill.

RUSSELL No, no, you can't—

LAMBERT It's my wedding anniversary! Right? *(To* **RICHARD***)* Send me their bill.

JULIE And his.

LAMBERT Send me both bills. Anyway... *(He embraces* **SUKI***)* It's for old time's sake as well, right?

SUKI Right.

RICHARD See you again soon?

MATT Absolutely.

SONIA See you again soon.

PRUE Absolutely.

SONIA Next celebration?

JULIE Absolutely.

LAMBERT Plenty of celebrations to come. Rest assured.

MATT Plenty to celebrate.

LAMBERT Dead right.

> **MATT** *slaps his thighs.*

MATT Like – who's in front? Who's in front?

> **LAMBERT** *joins in the song, slapping his thighs in time with* **MATT**.

LAMBERT AND MATT
>   WHO'S IN FRONT?
>   WHO'S IN FRONT?

LAMBERT
>   GET OUT OF THE BLOODY WAY
>   YOU SILLY OLD CUNT.

> **LAMBERT** *and* **MATT** *laugh.*

> SUKI *and* RUSSELL *go to their table to collect handbag and jacket, etc.*

SUKI Sweet of him to take the bill, wasn't it?

RUSSELL He must have been very fond of you.

SUKI Oh, he wasn't all that fond of me really. He just liked my...oh, you know...

RUSSELL Your what?

SUKI Oh, my...you know...

LAMBERT Fabulous evening.

JULIE Fabulous.

RICHARD See you soon then.

SONIA See you soon.

MATT I'll be here for breakfast tomorrow morning.

SONIA Excellent!

PRUE See you soon.

SONIA See you soon.

JULIE Lovely to see you.

SONIA See you soon, I hope.

RUSSELL See you soon.

SUKI See you soon.

> *They drift off.*

JULIE'S VOICE So lovely to meet you.

SUKI'S VOICE Lovely to meet you.

> *Silence.*
>
> *The* WAITER *stands alone.*

WAITER When I was a boy my grandfather used to take me to the edge of the cliffs and we'd look out to sea. He bought me a telescope. I don't think they have telescopes anymore. I used to look through this telescope and sometimes I'd see a boat. The boat would grow bigger through the telescopic lens. Sometimes I'd see people on the boat. A man, sometimes, and a woman, or sometimes two men. The sea glistened.

My grandfather introduced me to the mystery of life and I'm still in the middle of it. I can't find the door to get out. My grandfather got out of it. He got right out of it. He left it behind him and he didn't look back.

He got that absolutely right.

And I'd like to make one further interjection.

He stands still.

Slow fade.

THIS IS NOT THE END

**Visit samuelfrench.co.uk
and discover the best
theatre bookshop
on the internet**

A vast range of plays
Acting and theatre books
Gifts

samuelfrench.co.uk
samuelfrenchltd
samuel french uk

www.ingramcontent.com/pod-product-compliance
Ingram Content Group UK Ltd.
Pitfield, Milton Keynes, MK11 3LW, UK
UKHW021848210426
5322IPUK00022B/538